Windy Weather

Written by Jillian Powell

Wayland

The Weather

Rainy Weather
Snowy Weather
Sunny Weather
Windy Weather

First published in 1992 by

Wayland (Publishers) Ltd

61, Western Road, Hove

East Sussex BN3 1JD, England

© Copyright 1992 Wayland (Publishers) Ltd

Series Editor: Francesca Motisi
Editor: Hazel Songhurst
Designer: Joyce Chester

British Library Cataloguing in Publication Data
  Powell, Jillian
  Windy Weather. – (Weather Series)
  I. Title II. Series
  551.5

  ISBN 0-7502-0506-7

Typeset by Dorchester Typesetting Group Ltd
Printed in Italy by G. Canale and C.S.p.A
Bound in Belgium by Casterman, S.A.

Contents

Words that appear in **bold** in the text are explained in the glossary on page 30

The wind and us

We always notice the weather when it's windy. Just walking in a strong wind can be hard work. Hats may blow away and umbrellas turn inside out.

In towns, dust and litter blow about. In the country, wind shakes the trees, bringing down leaves and branches. Do you like windy weather?

Windy days are ideal for kite flying. Kites are designed to catch the wind, so each gust sends them soaring and diving in the sky. Playing ball sports, like tennis, can be difficult when the wind is blowing. Can you play your favourite sport in windy weather?

Wind and weather

Air moves when it warms up or cools down. We call this moving air the wind. Winds carry rain and warmth round the world and produce the weather. They cool the world's hottest lands and bring warmth to the coldest. Knowing which way the wind is blowing helps us to know what kind of weather to expect.

When the wind is blowing, the air feels cooler. A gentle breeze on a hot summer's day can be pleasantly cooling, but in winter, strong winds can make it feel bitterly cold. This is called **wind chill**. Wind-proof clothes such as 'wind-cheater' anoraks, hats, scarves and gloves help keep us warm in cold windy weather.

The energy of the wind

Have you noticed how washing
dries faster on a windy day?
Wind blows against the clothes,

shaking out some of the water.
As more water **evaporates**
from the surface of the clothes,
wind blows away the water
vapour. The wind is blowing
against these flags making
them flutter in the air.

Windy weather can cause problems. Strong winds make the sea rough, endangering small fishing and pleasure boats. People travelling by ferry or passenger liner may suffer sea-sickness. When winds reach **gale** force, fishing boats may be unable to set out, and ferries may be cancelled.

Measuring the wind

Weather forecasters use **satellite** pictures, like the one below, and weather balloons to help forecast wind speed and direction.

Regular shipping forecasts are broadcast to give warnings of gales at sea. People who work outdoors, such as farmers and builders, also need warning of strong winds. Can you think of any other jobs affected by windy weather?

The **windsock** in the picture is used to show
the speed and direction of the wind. Windsocks
are used at airports, seaports and on exposed
roads. People using cars, high-sided lorries,
boats or bicycles must all take extra care in
windy weather. Pilots try to avoid strong
headwinds which can slow down an aircraft.

Wind sports

The yachts in the picture are using the power of the wind by catching it in their sails. Large sailing ships once carried people and goods all over the world. Today cargo and cruise ships are powered by oil, and sailing is mostly for sport and pleasure.

Windsurfers use the power of the wind to travel over the waves for fun! The windsurfer holds on to the sail frame, steering it so that the sail catches the wind and pushes the sail board along over the water.

Wind and flight

Winds can carry hot-air balloons many kilometres. People travel in a basket underneath the balloon, either for sport or to take **aerial** photographs. Glider aircraft and hang-gliders also use warm air currents and winds to stay in the air.

Birds use warm air currents and winds when flying. Eagles soar high on rising currents of warm air. Birds that **migrate** such as swallows, use winds to help them reach their summer breeding grounds or winter homes. These photographs show a flock of flamingoes and a bald eagle soaring on air currents.

Insects, plants and the wind

The wind can help small insects travel long distances. Tiny spiders and caterpillars climb plant stems then throw silken threads into the wind, so that they can glide from plant to plant. In hot countries, swarms of locusts travel with the wind, to find food and lay their eggs.

The wind helps plants to reproduce by carrying pollen and seeds. Some plant seeds, like dandelions, are shaped like tiny parachutes (right), so that they float easily through the air. Others, like the sycamore seeds (above), have wings which help them spin and glide along.

Protection against the wind

People have found different ways of protecting
their homes against strong winds. This house
has shutters to protect windows and keep out
draughts. Lines of trees, or tall hedges can be
planted to act as windbreaks for houses and
gardens, or to protect crops.

In countries where winter winds can be bitterly cold, some animals and birds are adapted to stay warm. Polar bears, which live in the **Arctic**, have thick fur with a layer of fat underneath to protect them. **Antarctic** penguins have a layer of fat under their closely-packed feathers. Other animals hide in burrows or hibernate to survive the winter.

Wind damage

In coastal areas, high winds can drive huge waves on to land, flooding streets and homes.

Low-lying land needs the protection of sea defences, such as strong sea walls.

Gales are strong winds that can uproot trees, lift house roofs and bring down power lines. People may be killed as boats are lost in rough seas, trees fall across roads and homes are wrecked. The village (above) in Bangladesh was destroyed by a fierce **cyclone**.

Wind and pollution

Chemicals in fumes from industrial plants (above), power stations and car exhausts travel up into the air and dissolve in rainwater, becoming acid rain. The wind can blow pollution from one country to make acid rain in another country. This can kill trees, poison lakes and damage crops.

Winds can spread forest fires after long periods of hot, dry weather. Flames and sparks fanned by the wind spread easily through dry wood and undergrowth. Foresters sometimes cut broad tracks, or firebreaks, through a forest to prevent fires spreading.

Monsoons and hurricanes

Some parts of the world have seasonal winds, called **monsoons**. For part of the year, the winds blow from the land, bringing dry weather. They change direction with the season, blowing warm, moist air from the sea and bringing rain. These pictures show rainy monsoon weather in Sri Lanka.

This funnel-shaped wind is a tornado and it can destroy whatever is in its path. In the Caribbean, the Far East and Australia, very strong winds called **hurricanes**, **typhoons** or cyclones can wreck towns and villages, ruin crops, and kill people and animals.

Wind and the landscape

Wind can shape the landscape, moving sand and loose soil around and wearing away rock faces. In exposed places, trees and plants may be bent in the direction of **prevailing winds**.

In **deserts** (top) wind creates ripples, **dunes** and hills. Rocks may be carved into strange shapes by winds driving sand and grit against them.

Wind causes **blizzards** in snowy weather, like this one in a Canadian town. Snow is whipped up into swirling snowstorms and it is hard to see.

Mountaineers and hill walkers may lose their way in a blizzard. Wind can drive heavy snow into deep **drifts**, which may block roads and trap sheep out in the fields.

Wind power

Windmills, like those in the picture, were widely used before the introduction of steam and oil power. The wind turned the sails, working machinery inside the mill. In flat, low-lying countries like the Netherlands, windmills were used to pump water from the fields into canals so crops would not be ruined. They were also used to grind wheat into flour.

Today, windpower can provide the world with a renewable source of energy. The picture shows a windfarm in California, USA. The windmills drive **turbines** which make electricity. Some people think windfarms look ugly. Others argue that they are good things to have because they provide energy without waste or harmful pollution. What do you think?

Glossary

Aerial   From the air.

Antarctic   Cold land mass around the South Pole.

Arctic   Cold land and seas around the North Pole.

Blizzards   Winter storms, with strong winds blowing loose snow.

Deserts   Dry regions on earth.

Drifts   Deep mounds of snow piled up by the wind.

Dunes   Mounds of sand heaped up by the wind.

Evaporate   When liquid (e.g. water) turns into vapour (tiny droplets in the air).

Gale   Wind strong enough to cause damage.

Headwind   Wind blowing from an opposite direction.

Hurricanes   Very violent storms, blowing at over 150 kilometres an hour. Also called **cyclones**, **typhoons**.

Migrate   To travel from one place to another.

Monsoons   Winds that change direction with the seasons and may bring rain.

Prevailing winds   Winds that blow steadily from one direction.

Satellite   A spacecraft that circles Earth and sends back weather pictures and reports.

Turbines   Motors driven by water, gas, steam or wind.

Wind chill   When a cold wind chills the body.

Windsock   A cone of fabric tied to a pole that shows wind speed and direction.

Books to read

Bramwell, Martyn **Weather** (Franklin Watts 1987)

Gribbin, John and Gribbin, Mary **Weather** (Macdonald 1985)

Lambert, David and Hardy, Ralph **Weather and its Work** (Orbis 1988)

Lambert, David **The Work of The Wind** (Wayland 1983)

Potter, Tony **BBC Factfinders Weather** (BBC Books 1989)

Taylor, Barbara **Wind and Weather** (Franklin Watts 1991)

Notes for parents and teachers

This series looks at four aspects of the weather with an interesting and informative approach. The specially chosen photographs reflect the author's innovative style involving the children directly with the subject. The clear and straight-forward text allows children to use the books independently, as a means for reference and as a resource.

All the books in the series relate closely to the National Curriculum offering support to any child embarking on Key Stage 2. Yet those children exploring the weather at home, can enjoy the many exciting ideas and photographs that invite discussion and question from any child.

Suggestions for extension activities

1 Keep a diary for a week, recording the daily wind speed and direction in your area. Find these out by listening to the radio weather forecast, watching it on TV, or by looking in a newspaper. Which day was the windiest?

2 Find out how people used wind power in the past. Do you think it was a useful form of energy? Do you think we could use it to make the power we need today?

3 Think of as many words as you can for windy weather. Use them in a story or a poem about a windy day.

Picture acknowledgements
The publishers would like to thank the following for allowing their photographs to be reproduced in this book: Brian and Cherry Alexander 27; CEPHAS 16, 18, 20 (below), 21 (below), 28; Bruce Coleman Ltd 5 (below, Thomas Buchholz), 10 (right, Jane Burton), 15 (inset, Johnny Johnson), 16 (below, Jane Burton); Eye Ubiquitous 4 (Paul Seheult), 7 (below, John Hulme), 11 (A. Carroll), 24 (above, L. Fordyce, below); ECOSCENE 20 (Cooper/above); Chris Fairclough 6, 7 (above); 8 (above); 26 (middle, below); Reflections Photo Library *cover* (Jennie Woodcock); Tony Stone 9, 12, 13, 14, 15 (main), 17 (above), 22, 23, 25; ZEFA 8 (main), 10 (left), 19, 26 (top).

Index